What Is a Desert?

by Mary Evans

Harcourt

Orlando   Boston   Dallas   Chicago   San Diego

Visit *The Learning Site!*

www.harcourtschool.com

What is a desert?

A desert is a place where it hardly ever rains. There are deserts all over the world.

Some deserts get only one or two inches of rain or snow a year. Other deserts get ten or twelve inches a year, at the most.

Most plants need much more rain than that to survive. Most animals need water to survive, as well. So, a desert is a place where only plants and animals that do not need a lot of water can live.

What do deserts look like?

Some deserts are sandy and hot. The wind blowing over the sand makes it ripple like waves on the ocean. The sand waves change as the wind blows. Any tracks in the sand quickly disappear.

Some deserts are rocky and cold. This rock formation is in Monument Valley. Do you think the rock looks like a monument? An admiring visitor passing through this place thought so and gave the valley its name. Monument Valley is part of the Painted Desert, in the states of Utah and Arizona.

Some deserts are very high. This photo was taken in a high part of the Painted Desert, in Arizona. The Painted Desert got its name because it is very colorful. Minerals give the sand and rock their pink, red, orange, and brown colors. Shadows make the colors look darker.

Some deserts are very low. Death Valley is the lowest place in California. It is the lowest place in North America. In fact, it's the lowest place in the whole Western Hemisphere.

This desert has arches of stone. These arches were carved by wind and sand. It took a very, very long time to make them.

Some deserts even have rivers flowing through them. Did you ever imagine a desert could look like this? There is very little rain here, but this river brings water from the mountains far away. Animals can drink the water. The water from the river also helps plants grow.

What is Death Valley like?

It gets hotter in Death Valley than in any other place in the United States. It's always dry there, too. In an average year, Death Valley gets only 2 inches of rain. In summer, temperatures reach 125°F during the day.

In winter, the weather is more pleasant. It's about 70°F in the daytime and drops to 40°F or lower at night.

If you want to see Death Valley, be choosy about when you go. Go in the winter, and keep your water jug nearby!

How did Death Valley get its name?

When the gold rush started in 1849, a small group of people left Utah for the gold fields of California. They trudged across the harsh Mojave Desert, with its scorching heat and lack of water. Many of the people died of thirst and the heat.

The survivors who finally reached the other side of the mountains were in no mood for celebrations. They named the desert valley they had just left "Death Valley." It has kept its name to this day.

Are there monsters in the desert?

Yes, there are! The Gila monster is a lizard that lives in the deserts of the southwestern United States. It grows to be about 20 inches long. It is the only poisonous lizard in the United States.

Like many other desert animals, the Gila monster stays in the shade during the day and hunts after dark, when it is cool. It eats small rodents, other lizards, and the eggs of birds and other reptiles.

When food is hard to find, the Gila
monster can go for months without eating.
It lives off the fat that it stores in its tail.

You won't find Gila monsters easily. There
aren't many of these slow-moving, peaceful
lizards left in the deserts. Many people like to
hunt them. In Arizona, there are laws against
hunting Gila monsters. These laws keep the
Gila monster from becoming extinct.

Are there other kinds of lizards in the desert?

Yes. During the day, there seem to be more lizards than any other kind of animal.

One lizard, the Tuscan banded gecko, has a surprising way to escape from danger. If a predator grabs the gecko by the tail, the gecko lets go of its tail. Then it runs off, leaving its wiggling tail behind for the predator to eat!

Another lizard sometimes looks like a tiny dinosaur. When the collared lizard wants to move fast, it stands up on its hind legs and runs like a tyrannosaurus!

One desert lizard has no ears. It is the greater earless lizard. But insects should beware! This lizard moves fast, and insects are its favorite food.

The chuckwalla has a special way to protect itself. This lizard blows up its stomach

to twice its size. It tries to make itself look bigger and more dangerous than it really is. This can trick an enemy into looking for smaller prey.

Why do cactuses look so strange?

Some desert cactuses look like monsters, too! They have adapted to the hot, dry land.

Cactuses have many spines sticking out of their thick green skin. The sharp spines help shade the cactus. They also help protect the cactus from being eaten.

Cactuses' thick skin keeps water from evaporating, or drying up. Like other cactuses, this barrel cactus stores up water for dry times. Animals can use this water, too.

Desert birds like the Gila woodpecker build their nests in the tall saguaro cactus. The saguaro makes shade for other desert animals, too. This cactus takes about 50 years to grow 6 feet tall. Sadly, people are taking away the land where it grows. There are fewer saguaros than there used to be.

Insects, birds, animals, and humans eat the fruit of the prickly pear cactus. Insects and birds also feed on the beautiful flowers of cactuses like the pincushion and claret cup.

Can eggs that are 100 years old hatch?

Scientists think they can. They know that eggs that are 25 years old can hatch.

In 1955, a heavy rain fell on a dry, dusty place called Bicycle Dry Lake in the Mojave Desert. There had been no water there for 25 years. In a few hours, the heavy rain formed a shallow lake. Two days later it was filled with newly hatched shrimp.

The shrimp eggs were laid 25 years before, when the last rainstorm formed a lake there. Then the lake dried up. The eggs had been in the dry soil all those years. Then, as soon as there was water again, the eggs hatched.

These shrimp have a very short life cycle. They hatch, grow up, mate, and lay eggs before the lake can dry up again.

Scientists think these shrimp eggs will wait even 100 years for the next rain or other water.

Bicycle Dry Lake
Mojave Desert

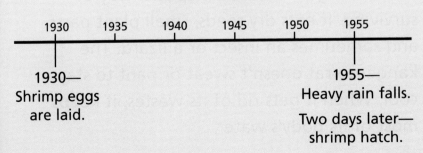

| 1930 | 1935 | 1940 | 1945 | 1950 | 1955 |

1930—
Shrimp eggs
are laid.

1955—
Heavy rain falls.

Two days later—
shrimp hatch.

How do desert animals survive?

It is very hot in the desert during the day. Most animals stay in underground burrows or caves or in the shade of desert plants. This keeps them from getting too hot and losing too much water.

The kangaroo rat has a special way of surviving. It eats dry seeds, small plant parts, and sometimes an insect or a lizard. The kangaroo rat doesn't sweat or pant to stay cool. When it gets rid of its wastes, it keeps most of its body's water.